MOOSE

# LIVING WILD

Published by Creative Education
P.O. Box 227, Mankato, Minnesota 56002
Creative Education is an imprint of The Creative Company
www.thecreativecompany.us

Design and production by Mary Herrmann
Art direction by Rita Marshall
Printed by Corporate Graphics in the United States of America

Photographs by Alamy (Blickwinkel, georgesanker.com, Hemis, MARKA, Sean O'Neill, Vova Pomortzeff), Corbis (Joel W. Rogers), Dreamstime (Aiok, Ivan Cholakov, Cumulus, Devangelisto, Jesper Elgaard, Caleb Foster, Andreas Gradin, Imagestar, Juliebuehler, Keith Livingston, Mesquite53, Shawn Milne, Malissa Parker, Ann Piaia, Sburel, Reinhard Tiburzy, Twildlife), Getty Images (CBS Photo Archive, John Eastcott and Yva Momatiuk, Eastcott Momatiuk, Jeff Foott, Raymond Gehman, Robert C Nunnington), iStockphoto (Andrey Artykov, Hank Bentiage, Suzann Julien, Roman Krochuk, Rich Legg, Lu McGowan, Philip Puleo, Eliza Snow, Paul Tessier, Michael Thompson)

Library of Congress Cataloging-in-Publication Data
Gish, Melissa.
Moose / by Melissa Gish.
p. cm. — (Living wild)
Includes bibliographical references and index.
Summary: A look at moose, including their habitats, physical characteristics such as their imposing antlers, behaviors, relationships with humans, and secure status in the world today.
ISBN 978-1-58341-973-1
1. Moose—Juvenile literature. I. Title. II. Series.

QL737.U55G57 2010
599.65'7—dc22     2009025174

CPSIA: 120109 PO1092
First Edition
9 8 7 6 5 4 3 2 1

**C** CREATIVE EDUCATION

# MOOSE

Melissa Gish

It is early September in Alaska's Kachemak Bay State Park.

The air is crisp with the promise of snow.

I t is early September in Alaska's Kachemak Bay State Park. The air is crisp with the promise of snow. In a shallow swamp, twin baby moose—just 3 months old and weighing nearly 200 pounds (91 kg) each—nibble on the twigs of an elderberry shrub. The tall grass rustles, and the moose look up from their browsing. The dark figure of a wolf emerges and steps toward the twins. Although

it is half the size of a baby moose, the wolf has sharp teeth and strong jaws. The twins, sensing danger, begin squealing. Almost immediately, the mother moose crashes violently through the branches to stand between the wolf and her offspring. The wolf freezes as the mother moose bellows and prepares to charge. A lone wolf is no match for a full-grown moose. Whirling around, the wolf disappears in a flash of gray fur, leaving the moose family to continue its browsing.

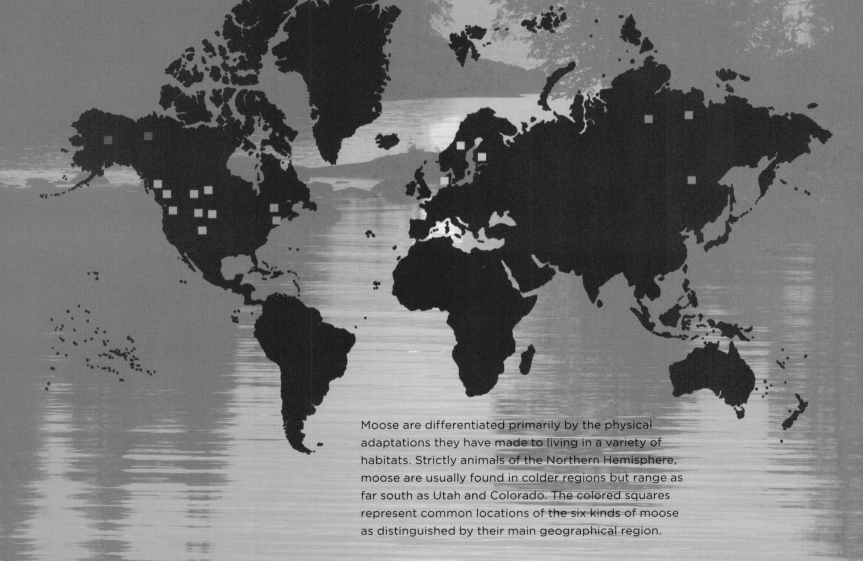

## WHERE IN THE WORLD THEY LIVE

■ **Yukon-Alaska Moose**
Alaska, Canadian Yukon Terriory

■ **Wyoming Moose**
Wyoming, Montana, Idaho, Utah, Colorado, Washington, Alberta, British Columbia

■ **Western Canadian Moose**
western and central Canada, north-central United States

■ **Eastern Canadian Moose**
eastern Canada, northeastern United States

■ **European Moose**
Scandinavia

■ **Siberian Moose**
Russia, Siberia, northern China

Moose are differentiated primarily by the physical adaptations they have made to living in a variety of habitats. Strictly animals of the Northern Hemisphere, moose are usually found in colder regions but range as far south as Utah and Colorado. The colored squares represent common locations of the six kinds of moose as distinguished by their main geographical region.

## EATER OF TWIGS

T he moose is the largest member of the Cervidae, or deer, family. There are six "subspecies" of moose, each named for the location of its habitat but not indicative of **genetic** differences from the main species. The Yukon-Alaska moose is found in Alaska and the Canadian Yukon Territory. The Wyoming moose—also known as the Shiras moose, for the early 20th-century wildlife photographer George Shiras III—is found in the western states of Wyoming, Montana, Idaho, Utah, Colorado, and Washington, as well as in southwestern Alberta and southeastern British Columbia in Canada.

The Western Canadian moose ranges throughout western and central Canada, as well as northern North Dakota, Minnesota, and Michigan. The Eastern Canadian moose lives in eastern Canada and the northeastern United States. The European moose is found primarily in the Scandinavian countries of Finland, Sweden, and Norway, while the Siberian moose lives in Russia, Siberia, and northern China, with isolated populations in Poland and the Czech Republic.

*Moose feed along a browse line, or an area six to eight feet (1.8–2.4 m) off the ground.*

**Male moose have larger humps on their shoulders than females because they have stronger muscles to support the weight of their antlers.**

*Elk, also called wapiti, are smaller than moose and can be found in herds containing as many as 400 animals.*

The word "moose" is taken from various words such as *moosh*, *mus*, and *moosu*, which, in the languages of some American Indians and Canadian First Nations of northeastern North America, refer to the moose's practice of stripping and eating twigs and bark. Moose are known as elk in Europe, from their German name, *elch*.

Despite being related to one another, deer, elk (the second-largest member of the deer family), and moose all vary in appearance. There are dozens of deer species, from South America's 22-pound (10 kg) southern pudu—the smallest deer in the world—to the common white-tailed deer of North America, to the reindeer of the frozen Arctic tundra. Moose, with their distinctive features, are rarely confused with other members of the Cervidae family.

Moose are mammals. All mammals produce milk to feed their young and, with the exceptions of the egg-laying platypuses and echidnas of Australia, give birth to live offspring. Mammals are also warm-blooded. This means that their bodies try to maintain a healthy, constant temperature that is usually warmer than their surroundings. Moose have two layers of fur to keep them warm in their cold northern habitats. Close to the body

*The dewlap hanging from a moose's neck is called* mousomodai, *meaning "moose bottle" in the language of the Iroquois.*

*Moose ears are 60 times larger than human ears and can pivot independently to pick up sounds from all directions.*

is a coat of thick, curly underfur. On top of the underfur are long, coarse guard hairs. These hairs are hollow and can trap warm air to provide the moose with **insulation** from the cold. The color of moose hair varies from light brown, to dark brown, to almost black.

The Yukon–Alaska moose lives in the coldest climate and is the largest of the species. A male moose, called a bull, of this subspecies may grow to stand more than seven feet (2.1 m) tall at the shoulder. A moose's weight **fluctuates** with the seasons, as the animal adds bulk in summer when food is plentiful and loses weight in winter when food is scarce. At full mass, a Yukon–Alaska bull moose averages 1,400 pounds (635 kg). A female, called a cow, is about the same height as a bull, but she is not as bulky and therefore weighs only about 800 pounds (363 kg).

The two subspecies of Canadian moose stand about 6.5 feet (2 m) tall at the shoulder. Bulls weigh about 1,300 pounds (590 kg). Bull European and Siberian moose are slightly smaller, standing about 6 feet (1.8 m) tall at the shoulder and weighing about 1,200 pounds (544 kg). About the same height as the European and Siberian moose, the Shiras moose is the slenderest moose species. These moose

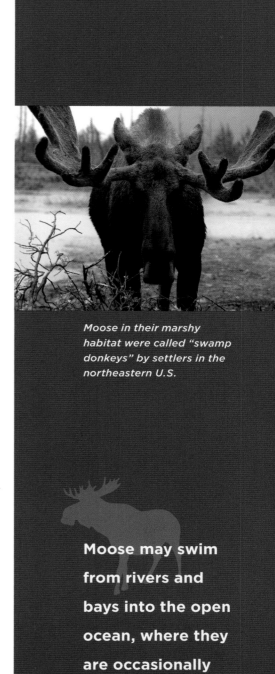

*Moose in their marshy habitat were called "swamp donkeys" by settlers in the northeastern U.S.*

**Moose may swim from rivers and bays into the open ocean, where they are occasionally attacked by killer whales.**

*European moose have shorter skulls and sharper teeth than North American moose, enabling them to feed on harder bark.*

live in climates that are not as cold and snowy, so they do not require as much mass as the other subspecies.

Large moose have large antlers, and smaller moose have smaller antlers. Antlers are **appendages** that grow from the top of the skull. A pair of antlers is called a rack. Antlers are sometimes confused with horns. Horns are made of bone covered with a hard tissue called keratin— the same substance that makes up human fingernails. Goats, sheep, and many other hoofed animals have horns that never fall off, unless they are broken.

Antlers appear only on bull moose and begin as little knobs called pedicles in the spring of each year. As the antlers grow, their shape becomes more complex, and a number of prongs develop. European moose differ from North American moose in the shape of their antlers. North American moose antlers have four prongs, and each individual antler can be divided into two lobes, like the wings of a butterfly. European moose have three prongs, and each individual antler has only a single lobe.

A layer of soft tissue called velvet covers the developing antlers and helps them grow throughout the summer. The velvet is filled with blood vessels that provide nutrients to

*In his first year, a bull calf may develop small "button antlers" from bumps known as antler buds.*

the growing antlers. By autumn, when the antlers have reached their full size, the velvet begins to dry up and loosen from the bone beneath it. Moose rub their antlers against trees to shed the velvet. The antlers then fall off in early winter, well after the mating season. The process of antler development, velvet shedding, and antler growth begins again every spring, with the antlers growing faster and larger each year. A rack may reach more than 6 feet (1.8 m) across from tip to tip and weigh up to 75 pounds (34 kg) by the end of a moose's life.

Moose require 45 to 60 pounds (20.4– 27.2 kg) of plants for food per day. A moose has 8 sharp teeth used

for tearing at grass and shrubs and 24 square, ridged teeth for grinding up twigs and bark. Digesting such woody food takes a special stomach—one with four chambers, or sections. Food passes through the first chamber, called the rumen, where bacteria and acids soften it. Then the food is regurgitated, or brought back up to the mouth. This food mass, called a cud, is chewed again. When it is swallowed, the cud passes through all four stomach chambers to be fully digested. Moose share this trait of cud chewing with cows, sheep, giraffes, llamas, bison, and many other hoofed mammals classified as ruminants.

*Some native peoples once collected moose antler velvet and boiled it to make a medicine to ease aching joints.*

*No other member of the deer family is able to automatically close its nostrils when dipping its head underwater.*

MELLOW TO MONSTROUS

Moose are not social animals, and they live alone for most of the year. They establish home ranges, or territories, as small as 1 square mile (2.6 sq km) or as large as 36 square miles (93 sq km). Moose usually select habitats that contain a mix of forest and wetland or streams. In spring, moose eat grasses and marsh plants such as horsetail and sedge, varieties of which exist in moose habitats around the world. In summer, they eat aquatic vegetation, including many varieties of pondweeds and milfoil. They can even dive 18 feet (5.5 m) underwater to reach the roots of water lilies at the bottom of a lake. They also eat the leaves of dozens of tree species, including such favorites as willow, birch, and aspen. In fall and winter, when **deciduous** trees have shed their leaves, moose eat twigs and bark.

Moose play a vital balancing role in the **food chains** of their habitats, preventing overgrowth of forests and swamps by eating selectively in large areas. Some moose may migrate seasonally from place to place, seeking better food sources. Others seldom stray from their home ranges except to travel to wintering grounds, where they gather

*Increasing daylight hours prompt antlers to grow quickly in the springtime.*

**When a moose dips its long nose underwater to feed on aquatic plants, its large nostrils automatically close, shutting out water.**

Brown bears, the second-largest predator on land (after polar bears), often choose to attack cows rather than bulls.

in groups to seek warmth and safety from their main predators: wolves and bears. Moose may travel 60 miles (97 km) or more to wintering grounds, following routes that were taught to them as youngsters by their mothers.

Moose are equipped with long legs and broad, cloven-hoofed feet that make travel through deep snow and muddy water possible. Cloven hooves are split into two parts called digits, which are similar to toes, and the skin between the digits is called the interdigital cleft. When moose walk through snow and water, they spread their digits apart, stretching the interdigital cleft and achieving an effect that is similar to a human walking on snowshoes through firmly packed snow. If the snow is only lightly compacted, moose can simply plow through it.

Sometimes moose get stuck in lightly packed snow that is too deep for them to raise their knees high enough to be able to push through it. This is a problem for many young, weak moose, which typically fall prey to predators. When attacked, a moose can deliver deadly kicks with its legs, seriously injuring and even killing its attackers. But if it is stuck in snow, a moose is helpless to defend itself.

Both black bears and grizzly bears attack and eat moose, although black bears typically target smaller moose. A bear bites a moose's neck to cut off its air supply and then devours it. Wolves hunt in groups called packs and bite at the legs and neck of the moose. Biting the legs cripples the moose, sending it tumbling to the ground, where the wolf pack can pounce on it. Humans hunt moose for trophies and food. Many people in rural areas rely on moose hunts each year to feed their families. Moose hunting season typically begins in the fall, when

*Moose have been known to travel to cities in search of trails and plowed roads in order to avoid deep snow.*

Antlers have a spongy, soft core that allows them to flex and absorb the shocks caused by mating-season battles.

normally even-tempered moose become aggressive in their search for mates.

Bull moose may leave their home ranges during mating season, a period called rut, in which they follow the scents and sounds of cows and become highly aggressive and intolerant of intruders. Bulls are in rut for two to three weeks in early fall. Moose are mature enough to mate when they reach about 18 months of age. Bulls and cows are drawn to each other by a strong scent emitted by the body and spread by the hairy dewlap, or bell, which dangles from the bottom of the neck. Moose also call to each other by making loud, bellowing sounds, called bugles, as they walk along flat meadows or the edges of swamps, where the sound can travel as far as two miles (3.2 km).

Because more mature males grow larger antlers, it is easy to tell which males will be the strongest breeders. Older bulls with larger antlers typically run off younger bulls with smaller antlers. Sometimes bulls of equal age will fight for the opportunity to mate with a cow. While battles to the death are rare, injuries and scars are common.

After a bull mates with one cow, he will leave her and seek other partners. After about a seven-and-a-half month

*After bugling to locate cows, a bull moose typically mates with two or three of them.*

**Researchers from Ontario's Guelph University found that a moose's antlers amplify sounds, helping bulls locate cows during mating season.**

*Moose calves grow faster than most mammals worldwide and are the fastest-growing big-game animals in North America.*

**gestation**, the pregnant female will find a secluded place to give birth. Cows have a greater than 50 percent chance of carrying twins, but triplets are rare. Baby moose, called calves, are born in May or June. A moose weighs an average of 30 pounds (13.6 kg) at birth. Its weight will increase by 10 times within the first 5 months of its life.

A calf is born with its eyes open. It is able to stand within a few hours of birth and immediately begins feeding on the milk produced by its mother. The calf is lighter colored than its mother, helping it blend in with its forested environment. After almost two weeks, the mother will take the calf into the forest or swamp to begin browsing for leaves and tender twigs. Although it eats vegetation all summer long, a calf depends on its mother's nutrient-rich milk for its first five months. The young moose's fur darkens, and in the fall, the mother will refuse to nurse it any longer. She may even chase it from her immediate area in order to force it to feed entirely on greenery.

A calf will remain with its mother through the winter months, but it will avoid contact with bulls, who occasionally view calves as threats to scarce food

supplies and try to kill them. When the calf reaches 12 months of age, it is called a yearling and must soon leave its mother's home range. The mother often chases her yearlings away shortly before she gives birth again. Calves and yearlings are the most susceptible to attacks by predators, and about 15 to 20 percent of moose die in their first year of life. Those that survive may live to be 20 years old.

*Calves stay close to their mothers as long as they can, remaining under her care and receiving milk.*

*Thousands-of-years-old petroglyphs, or images carved into rock, often depict animals and hunting scenes.*

# A TOWER OF COURAGE

The first humans to travel from Asia to North America did so by crossing the Bering **Land Bridge** about 12,000 years ago. They followed animals such as moose that had traveled the same route, and because of this, moose became a primary food source for many early inhabitants of far northern North America. **Archaeologists** have uncovered evidence suggesting that the large animals were often hunted in the water and on land. As early as 4000 B.C., hunters had devised a system that involved snaring moose as they walked along familiar trails. The hunters targeted moose without antlers so that the ropes of the snares could slip easily over their heads. A trapped moose could then be stabbed with primitive spears. In winter, these ancient hunters used a technique called crusting. Wearing primitive snowshoes, the hunters drove moose to places where the snow was deep and soft but crusted over with a thin layer of ice. The moose fell through the crust and became trapped in the deep snow. Ironically, the hunters' snowshoes were made of bent twigs tied with thin strips of moose hide.

**A nearly 6,500-year-old moose antler found by archaeologists in a Cree Indian burial site in 2001 is one of the oldest moose artifacts ever discovered.**

*Antlers shed by moose are often collected and sold as rustic decorations.*

**Toronto artist Charles Pachter displays several portraits of Queen Elizabeth II pictured with moose in his Moose Factory Gallery.**

When captured and killed, every part of a moose was used. American Indian hunters valued the spirit of the moose as well. The Cree hung moose antlers in trees so the moose's spirit could watch the sunrise and not be saddened by having given its life so that people could eat it. The Iroquois and Algonquin tribes of the Northeast hung strips of moose flesh in trees as a sign of gratitude to the animal. Even the bones were never discarded. Many were made into useful tools; others were arranged in neat piles to show respect for the animal.

To express the value that they placed on the moose, many groups of native North Americans included moose in petroglyphs, or rock carvings, and cave paintings. Such artifacts have been found from British Columbia to Maine. In Kejimkujik National Park in Nova Scotia, Canada, the Mi'kmaq (*MEEG-em-ach*) people depicted moose in the petroglyphs they created more than 2,000 years ago. Similar moose petroglyphs have also been found in Norway and Sweden.

The first Europeans to see moose in North America were early explorers such as Jacques Cartier, who discovered the St. Lawrence River in 1535 and claimed

*Ancient painted images called pictographs typically showcase important animals and their relationship to humans.*

In 2000, Toronto mayor Mel Lastman had 325 uniquely painted and decorated life-size sculptures of moose placed around the city.

Canadian land for France. Samuel de Champlain, another French explorer and the founder of Quebec City in Canada, wrote about his encounters with moose, calling them *orignal*, which means "moose" in French. This word was derived from the word *orenac*, or deer, which is what a community of **Basque** fishermen who were living in Canada called the animal. The Irish poet Thomas Moore later chronicled a moose sighting in a poem describing his impressions of the St. Lawrence wilderness.

As 17th- and 18th-century European fur traders moved across North America, moose became an important commodity. The Hudson's Bay Company, the oldest **commercial corporation** in North America, relied heavily on both native and French trappers and hunters to provide animal **pelts** that could be sold throughout the eastern U.S. and Europe. Small animals with valuable fur included beavers, otters, mink, and martens. But one of the most desired hides was that of the moose, which is reflected by two moose being the most prominent figures in the Hudson's Bay Company's **coat of arms**.

Clothing manufacturer Abercrombie & Fitch, founded in 1892, still bears a moose as its official logo. Canada's oldest independent brewery, Moosehead Breweries Limited, uses an image of a moose's head as its logo. The moose can also be seen on the U.S. state flags of Maine (where it is the official state animal) and Michigan, as well as on the coat of arms of Ontario, Canada. The moose is considered a towering symbol of integrity and courage, and it represents the tradition of valuing wilderness.

The moose proved its worth as an American symbol when, in 1786, French naturalist Georges-Louis Leclerc insulted the U.S. by writing that all of its wildlife was inferior to Europe's. As American Minister to France, Thomas Jefferson ordered that a moose skeleton, including a head with massive antlers, be sent to Paris, demonstrating that American moose were taller than European moose. Leclerc was forced to apologize for his statement, and Jefferson hung the moose's antlers in his home as a reminder of how impressive American wildlife was.

Beginning in the 1800s, people tried to domesticate, or tame, moose, training them to pull carts and wagons and riding them like horses. This trend faded as people realized that moose cannot survive long in captivity.

**A 32-foot-tall (10 m) and 10-ton (9,000 kg) statue known as Mac the Moose greets visitors to Moose Jaw, Saskatchewan, Canada.**

*Moose have a prehensile upper lip that is able to grasp plant matter.*

**Mick E. Moose is the official mascot of the Manitoba Moose, an American Hockey League team headquartered in Winnipeg, Canada.**

They are picky eaters and get depressed when confined, so they require large areas of vegetation in which to remain occupied. Only two major moose farms remain in operation for the purposes of producing milk and conducting moose research. One is located in Kostroma Oblast, Russia, and the other is in Bjurholms, Sweden, where moose cheese is also produced.

An aggravated moose appeared in two early Walt Disney cartoons, establishing the moose's reputation as a fearsome forest giant. *The Moose Hunt* (1931) was the first cartoon to introduce the character of Mickey Mouse's pet dog Pluto, and *Moose Hunters* (1937) depicted an angry moose chasing Goofy and Donald Duck through the forest. In the 1950s and '60s, the television show *Captain Kangaroo* presented a mischievous moose named Mr. Moose; he was a master of knock-knock jokes.

In the 1990s, viewers of the television show *Northern Exposure* saw a moose in the show's opening credits each week. The symbol of the fictional small town's traditionally laid-back attitude was named Mort. Perhaps the most famous TV moose was Bullwinkle J. Moose, who starred with his best friend Rocky J. Squirrel in

two popular cartoon series from 1959 through 1964. Bullwinkle was created by Jay Ward and Alex Anderson. In 2000, Universal Pictures released the computer-animated film, *The Adventures of Rocky and Bullwinkle*, keeping Bullwinkle J. Moose alive for another generation of moose fans to enjoy.

*The moose that appeared in* Northern Exposure *belonged to a captive herd at Washington State University.*

*Shiras moose migrate from higher altitudes in summer to lower elevations, where browsing is less difficult, in winter.*

## MANY, MANY MOOSE

In most forests and wetlands where moose exist, moose populations are healthy. Moose are not considered an endangered species; in fact, in some places, moose are overly abundant and must be managed with environmental programs to control their numbers. Throughout the history of mammals, the moose has remained a highly successful species.

The earliest ancestors of the deer family appeared about 40 million years ago. These were called pseudo-deer because they had horns instead of antlers. As these animals' horns slowly **evolved** into true antlers, the pseudo-deer became proto-deer, or "first deer." Proto-deer existed about 20 million years ago and evolved into many types of deer, elk, and moose. *Libralces gallicus*, the earliest known ancestor of the moose, lived in central Europe two million years ago. About one million years later, the larger *Libralces latifrons* evolved and spread across Europe and Russia. It had a thick neck, and its antlers were positioned on the sides of the skull, growing straight outward. Its broad rack stretched 8.5 feet (2.6 m) from tip to tip, and each single-lobed antler curved slightly upward like a dish.

*After shedding their long winter coats in the spring, moose look more like their deer cousins.*

**Moose feces appear as nuggets a little smaller than Tootsie Roll candies, and the average moose produces 380 of them per day.**

*Filled with air, a moose's hollow guard hairs help the animal stay afloat while swimming.*

**Moose's eyesight is only average, but their sense of smell is powerful, allowing moose to detect predators before they can see them.**

Scientists believe that *Libralces latifrons* traveled from Siberia to North America by crossing the Bering Land Bridge about 250,000 years ago. Once in North America, this animal spread across the land, evolving into several varieties suited to different environments. Fossil evidence shows that early moose extended as far south as South Carolina. These large moose eventually died out and were replaced by modern moose about 75,000 years ago.

Moose exist in varying numbers in many parts of the Northern Hemisphere. After Canada, with its population of more than 800,000, Sweden has the largest moose population, with about 250,000. Alaska is home to 150,000 moose, while Idaho claims 20,000 moose, and Oregon carefully monitors its stock of nearly 40 moose. Government agencies and universities conduct a number of research projects regarding moose populations, tracking the animals' movements and studying the effects of human activities and **global warming** on moose.

A natural moose laboratory exists at Isle Royale National Park, which encompasses an island in the northwestern corner of Lake Superior, near the lakeshore city of Copper Harbor, Michigan. Since 1958, the

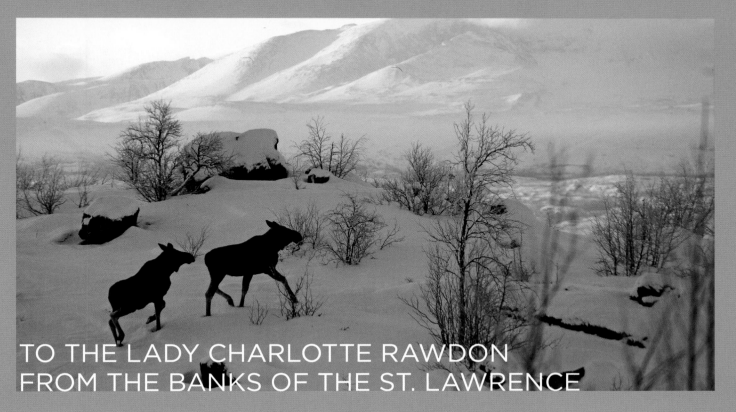

# TO THE LADY CHARLOTTE RAWDON
# FROM THE BANKS OF THE ST. LAWRENCE

Oft, when hoar and silvery flakes
Melt along the ruffled lakes,
When the gray moose sheds his horns,
When the track, at evening, warns
Weary hunters of the way
To the wig-wam's cheering ray,
Then, aloft through freezing air,
With the snow-bird soft and fair
As the fleece that heaven flings
O'er his little pearly wings,
Light above the rocks I play,

Where Niagara's starry spray,
Frozen on the cliff, appears
Like a giant's starting tears.
There, amid the island-sedge,
Just upon the cataract's edge,
Where the foot of living man
Never trod since time began,
Lone I sit, at close of day,
While, beneath the golden ray,
Icy columns gleam below,
Feather'd round with falling snow,

And an arch of glory springs,
Sparkling as the chain of rings
Round the neck of virgins hung,—
Virgins, who have wander'd young
O'er the waters of the west
To the land where spirits rest!

*From "To the Lady Charlotte Rawdon
from the Banks of the St. Lawrence,"
by Thomas Moore  (1779–1852)*

*Wolves usually wait to target a sick or injured moose and avoid attacking one that is healthy and strong.*

Isle Royale Wolf-Moose Study—the longest-running predator-prey study in the world—has been monitoring the relationship between moose and one of their major predators: eastern timber wolves. Moose took up residence on the island about 100 years ago when they either walked across the frozen lake or swam from nearby Canada. About 50 years later, wolves also walked over ice to the island. Both species became stranded and helped shape a new **ecosystem** on the island.

Researchers from Michigan Technological University

follow the natural cycle of life on the island: as the moose population increases, wolves have more to eat, and thus they thrive. But when the abundant wolves kill too many moose, food becomes scarce and wolves die off. The information gathered from this project is invaluable to scientists who manage wildlife around the world.

Moose are also studied in Minnesota, where climate change seems to have adversely affected their cold-weather-loving population. Over the past 40 years, the average winter temperature in northwestern Minnesota has increased by 12 °F (7.2 °C), causing severe stress on area moose, whose **mortality rate** there is three times higher than in any other part of the world. Scientists are concerned that the state's remaining 7,000 moose could disappear by 2050.

Warmer winter temperatures can make moose more vulnerable to diseases and **parasites**. One parasite is the meningeal worm, commonly called the brain worm, which grows in the moose's brain and spine, causing **paralysis** and death. There is no treatment for brain worm. Winter ticks are another serious problem. As many as 80,000 of these tiny bloodsuckers can live on a single moose, driving it to

*Alaskan moose produce the largest antlers when a bull is 10 to 12 years old.*

**According to Iroquois tradition, when the wind blew from the east, the people referred to it as "the moose spreading its breath."**

*A moose is safest from the dangers of cars and people when it is browsing in a remote, wooded area.*

scratch furiously on tree bark to relieve itching. Scratching all day instead of feeding can cause a moose to starve and weaken. Also, the loss of important insulating fur leaves moose vulnerable to the cold.

Some research involves managing overabundant moose. About 100 years ago in northern New York, moose had been overhunted and pushed out of their habitat, leaving only 50 to 100 moose in the state during the 1990s. Now, as moose are being pushed out of habitats in other northeastern states, they are returning to New York. With about 500 moose in the area, wildlife management officials must monitor the moose to keep them away from human-populated areas and educate the public about moose encounters, which are becoming more common.

The most hazardous type of human-moose interaction is on roadways. Moose crave salt, and in many northern cities, salt is used to melt ice on paved roadways, luring moose toward the roadways to lick the salt. Moose also cross roadways, which can be deadly for both motorists and moose. When a vehicle hits a moose, the animal's legs bend or break under the impact, and the moose's body is thrown into the vehicle's windshield. Each year, thousands of moose are killed by vehicles and trains—and dozens of people also die.

Many government agencies are responsible for monitoring moose populations and developing methods of reducing human–moose conflicts. In an effort to reduce train collisions with moose, Norway has set aside millions of dollars in funding to build fences along its national railroad system, clear vegetation away from the tracks, and create moose feeding areas away from the railroads. In the end, the cost of such ventures outweighs the expense of train wrecks and loss of human life.

Moose are a valuable part of Earth's northern wilderness areas. They offer cultural, educational, and economic value to humans, as thousands of moose hunting permits are sold all over North America and Europe, providing funds for many wildlife programs. Moose also help maintain the natural balance of their habitats by preventing overgrowth of vegetation and providing food for large predators. It is important for people who share these northern environments to respectfully manage both human and wildlife activities in order to maintain healthy ecosystems in which the noble moose can thrive.

*In 2008, the Canadian province of New Brunswick constructed tunnels for moose to travel under a highway.*

## ANIMAL TALE: THE MOOSE AND THE CATFISH

**The moose was considered a quietly noble creature by native peoples who shared their land with the animal. This story from the Menominee—one of the oldest tribes native to what is now Wisconsin—tells how the moose deals quietly but firmly with conflict among other creatures who share the marsh where he lives.**

Long ago, Moose spent his summer days munching on the manoomin, or wild rice, that grew in the marsh. Only the manoomin's flowers stood above the water, so Moose would pinch his nostrils shut, dip his head into the water, and curl his upper lip around the stalks, pulling them gently to the surface to chew them up.

Day after day, the catfish chief watched the moose step into the marsh and feed on the manoomin. "This moose is eating all of our grass," the catfish chief said to his tribe. "Soon it will all be gone."

A member of the catfish tribe looked puzzled. "Why should we care?" he said. "We do not eat the grass."

The catfish chief was stubborn, though. "This is *our* marsh, and that is *our* grass!" he snorted.

The members of the catfish tribe looked at each other, nodding their heads in agreement. "This is *our* marsh," they chanted, "and that is *our* grass!"

"Follow me," the chief said to his tribe. "We must drive the moose out of our marsh." And so the catfish chief and his tribe swam to the edge of the marsh. Slipping silently among the manoomin stalks, they waited for the moose to arrive.

When the sun climbed high in the sky, Moose appeared at the marsh. He stepped into the water and waded across the muddy bottom toward the manoomin. Just as he was about to dip his head into the water, he felt a sharp jab in his foot. The catfish chief had stabbed Moose with his spear.

Moose cried out in surprise. Lifting his foot from the water, Moose found the catfish chief gripping a long spear that was lodged in Moose's foot. "Why have you stabbed me?" Moose asked the catfish chief.

"This is *our* marsh, and that is *our* grass," replied the chief. "You must leave this place."

"But this land belongs to all of us," said Moose. "We can share. There is plenty for all."

"No!" cried the catfish chief. He pulled out his spear and flopped back into the water. Then he ordered his tribe to attack. All of the catfish began stabbing Moose's feet with their spears. Moose tried to escape, lifting one foot and then another, tromping through the mud until he was out of the marsh.

Then the catfish chief raised his head, which had been flattened by Moose's foot, above the water's surface. "Look what you have done!" he cried. Many of his tribe were dead, stomped by Moose, but some had managed to swim away.

"I am sorry, catfish chief," the moose said, "but you left me no choice." The catfish chief swam away, grumbling and clutching his spear.

And today, when you see catfish, you will see that they still carry their spears—the spines on their back fin and two front side fins—and they still have flat heads because Moose stomped them into the mud.

## GLOSSARY

**appendages** – parts that project from the main part of the body and have distinct functions

**archaeologists** – people who study human history by examining ancient peoples and their artifacts

**Basque** – of a people from northeastern Spain and southwestern France

**coat of arms** – the official symbol of a family, state, nation, or other group

**commercial corporation** – a business enterprise that seeks to gain a profit

**deciduous** – of a tree or shrub that sheds its leaves annually

**ecosystem** – a community of organisms that live together in an environment

**evolved** – gradually developed into a new form

**fluctuates** – rises and falls in an irregular number or amount

**food chains** – systems in nature in which living things are dependent on each other for food

**genetic** – relating to genes, the basic physical units of heredity

**gestation** – the period of time it takes a baby to develop inside its mother's womb

**global warming** – the gradual increase in Earth's temperature that causes changes in climates, or long-term weather conditions, around the world

**insulation** – the state of being protected from the loss of heat

**land bridge** – a piece of land connecting two landmasses that allowed people and animals to pass from one place to another

**mortality rate** – the number of deaths in a certain area or period

**paralysis** – loss of muscle movement

**parasites** – animals or plants that live on or inside another living thing (called a host) while giving nothing back to the host; some parasites cause disease or even death

**pelts** – the skins of animals with the fur or wool still attached

## SELECTED BIBLIOGRAPHY

Alaska Department of Fish and Game. "Moose." State of Alaska. http://www.adfg.state.ak.us/pubs/notebook/biggame/moose.php.

Franzmann, Albert W., Charles C. Schwartz, and Richard E. McCabe, eds. *Ecology and Management of the North American Moose.* Boulder: University Press of Colorado, 2007.

Geist, Valerius. *Moose: Behavior, Ecology, Conservation.* Osceola, Wisc.: Voyageur Press, 2005.

Mooseworld. "Homepage." http://www.mooseworld.com.

National Geographic. "Moose." Animals. http://animals.nationalgeographic.com/animals/mammals/moose.html.

Van Ballenberghe, Victor. *In the Company of Moose.* Mechanicsburg, Penn.: Stackpole Books, 2004.

Moose are so at home in the water that they can remain underwater for 30 seconds or more at a time.

**INDEX**